# NO
# NONSENSE

*A Millennials' Guide on How to Leave Your Parents House*

By Patrick Evans

# Dedication

To my Mother Theresa.

And my Girlfriend Jasmine whose Support has brought me to where I am today.

# Table of Content

# Introduction

It is a new world with new realities. So many things have changed, some at alarming rates. Our politics have become sophisticated, interpersonal relationships now transcend territorial borders, our lifestyles have new meanings and directions, and our daily activities are on new levels due to regular technological innovations and inventions. One thing not left out of this trend is how young people, particularly millennials, crave independence and therefore the rising wave of their emigration from their parents' houses and protection. From the extant socio-cultural patterns obtainable globally and with the current trend, it shows that leaving one's parents at a point in life to stay independently is always inevitable. There are needs and desires that are best satisfied or achieved while alone. We must at some points in our lives form other strong, meaningful relationships with others. We would meet the love of our lives. We would sometimes get married and have kids. The list goes on and on. What is important is, we would at a phase in our lives crave privacy and independence which transit us fully into adulthood.

It is however noteworthy that there are as many mistakes as the increased number of millennials transiting into independent living. Many millennials get it all wrong in how they go about this decision. Many make unavoidable and irredeemable mistakes that cost them their relationships, sanity and sadly lives. Some run into debts, some into crime, others into oblivion! Therefore, painstaking planning is key to a fulfilling transition. To achieve a smooth transition, it is best to sit on the shoulders of experienced people who have travelled that path and are willing to help new travelers avoid costly mistakes they made.

In this masterpiece, I am going to reveal to you my proven, step-by-step system that will help you ease into this rather ravenous journey of independent living. This guide covers really important things like how to handle your savings appropriately to little ones as what you should have with you as preparation for the first night in your new house. It is a comprehensive guide that covers arrays of issues, knowledge of which would make your transition easy and fruitful.

So, you have decided to move out? That's great! It is absolutely understandable. There comes a time in every human being's life when they must flee the nest and move on to greater things. Things unforeseeable when stuck in your 2-metre-wide bedroom at your Parent's house that is. It has to be understood that everyone has their lives to live and destiny to pursue. Leaving one's parents to stay alone is although a risky decision but it is a brave one key to individual tremendous successes and fulfilment. It opens your eyes to new realities and induces new habits, reasoning, lifestyle, preferences and so on.

I am 23 years of age, and fresh out the opposite side of life you are about to hop out from. It is seemingly easy to do but the great success lies in greater, in-depth planning. And the insights and guidelines are what you can get from my book which if learned by heart will solve bulk of the problems you will unavoidably face if you want to begin.

It's certainly not the head first!

I was 18 years old and had got my first job as a security guard in a local prison. I was doing well financially, and I saw potentials in myself. As you would expect, I spent the first year of my working life with my mother, having to wrap my head around her favourite anthem which she belabored millions of times, "Patrick, save your money!" "Patrick, you need to learn how to manage your money." I heard that a lot I began to have ideas on how to make it into a billboard hit song. I am sure it would not sell because it was going to be boring!

And then came the decision that changed everything for me so dramatically. It changed my whole life. The brave decision motivated me to write this book to serve as guidance to millennials who plan to take the same route or are even weary to decide. It is certainly a big decision to weary and it's therefore understandable that some fear to take the risk. It is inevitable. It should be planned, not feared.

I decided to move out!

Now, you know what? I can beat my chest with confidence that you have come this far, reading the book, because you are considering moving out, or you are a parent looking for guidance for your beloved bambino.

Interestingly, I dearly wish I could start this whole process all over again, right back to my first day as a security guard in prison, but with exactly the same knowledge I have today.

I wish I was a miracle worker to make this happen but unfortunately, I am not. But of course, what could be more beautiful than helping those in my old shoes take informed decisions and have the best start in life?

That is exactly the purpose of this book. I penned this to avail to you all the advice, hints and tips I garnered through my journey and really wish I could have given to myself. I really hope it will be of great help.

This brings me onto what I like to call the Immediate Reaction Phase.

This is a process which I regularly go through religiously and I have achieved very good results doing so.

This is the stage I have an idea come to mind, and thereafter sit and think about how it may alter my future and whether it will have positive or negative effects on myself and on others.

If I figure it is a beneficial move, I charge full steam ahead right at whatever the objective may be, and I do not relent at this until I have succeeded and achieved what I set out for.

For me, it brings immediate and, from my experience, the most rewarding results. It enables you to critically examine all angles to the situation, consider the possible problems and marshal the best solutions.

You should however carefully note this. This is not- and I repeat, it is not- how to go about making the decision to leave home.

But me being me, thinking I knew best, that was exactly what I did!

I had money, right?

I started the journey and within a week I was sitting on the living room floor of my very own rented house.

From that moment, I charged through everything, I made mistakes, I ignored people, I smashed through every obstacle like a bull in a china shop and the mess I had made was not good, whatsoever.

Three years on, and I am seated in Accident and Emergency talking to councilors about depression and suicidal thoughts. What happened in those three years put me through so much trauma and stress that I just wanted to run away from it all and never come back. I hated myself for leaving home and getting into this mess- a criminal record and thousands of pounds of debts were among the worst I faced. But eventually, I realized that it was my cross and I had to take responsibility and carry it alone. And that was the beginning of the rebirth.

I took charge, did all my research, approached people for help, used every resource I could possibly find to get myself into a position to clean up the carnage and begin to move forward.

And that is exactly what I did. Consequent upon the lessons I have learnt, I put together a strategy for getting my head above water and having a fresh start.

And once I was in the clear, I came up with another strategy for maintaining a happy and healthy lifestyle. That facilitated my progress and development into who I am today.

The man I once was has helped shape the man I am today. My purpose is to help make this the most enjoyable, stress-free experience as possible for you. If you are looking for a simple but detailed, step-by-step guide, this my No-Nonsense: A Millennials Guide for Moving out of Your Parents House is what you need!

# Step 1: Create Your Monthly Budget

Timing is the most important part of the whole process. It is so important that if you get it wrong or you rush into this process, you will end up in a ton of debt before you even begin. That is why it is important to sit and ask if you even need to leave yet and if you really do, you must plan the future well for you to be able to absolve any exigencies and eventually overcome it.

When you get a job, earning money and have decided that you can afford to kick-start the process, the very first thing to do is to work out your finances.

It is of the utmost importance that you possess fundamental knowledge on how well to manage your own finances. Without this basic financial management skills, running into debt is inevitable. Being in serious debt at that stage in your life is definitely not what you would wish for. It is agonizing and a harrowing experience. To avoid it, plan well.

In this chapter on finances, I explain in great detail how I successfully managed my finances and saved money and how that could assist you too on the journey.

First thing first, write down your monthly wage on a piece of paper.

Then halve it!

The 50 percent of your wage which should include your allowance of necessities should contain the following:

- Bills

- Rent/mortgage

- Food

- Transport

50 percent is used because that has to be space for savings.

The complete list looks like this:

- 50% Necessities

- 10% Long-term savings

- 10% Financial independence

- 10% Education

- 10% Fun

- 10% Gifts

It is imperative you separate your monthly wage by percentages and write them out in this fashion so that you can see in front of you a diagram of how much money you must spend on what objective. This way, it becomes easy and straightforward for you to track your finances.

By doing this, you will have the exact amount of money that you can afford to spend on each objective. I call it objective because that is a target or a maximum amount you have to set for yourself and above which you must not go. It must be kept as it is.

You should divide your monthly payout in this format and take a few months to get used to this process. Write a list if it helps.

You must only be allowing yourself to spend 10% of your wage on yourself for this time.

This process will familiarize you with the reality of the cost of living. The bright side, apart from teaching you the habit of accountability, is you save more. It is even great if you begin this while you are still under the roof and protection of your parents. You will be able to save up to about 90 percent of your income which you can thereafter use to rent an apartment. It also gives you time to make and correct your mistakes and, of course, learn self-restraint

1.      Emergency savings

What is key to an effective financial management system is well-planned savings. They are very important. It is a safety net that allows you survive the rainy days so much so that if the worst-case scenario lands at your feet and you lose your job, you must have 3-9 months of emergency savings stored away to allow yourself breathing time, and time to search for a new job. If this is not available in such trying times, life could really be bad.

2.      Long-term savings

A wise man once told me that by spending your money on things other than your actual needs, you are taking away from your future. What this translates to is whenever you want children and a marriage, you will be struggling then just as you are right now. I wonder why anyone will want to live the same way hustling, for the rest of their lives. It just doesn't make sense.

By putting 10% of your wages in a Savings Account in your bank, you are paying money to your future self- when you would want a car, or a bigger house, or even a family holiday. Those things will never ever happen if you don't start preparing for them now. It is not rocket science- you reap whatever you sow.

## 3.     Financial independence

You need another Savings account for this. You also deposit in here every month 10 percent of your wages.

This is the money you will use to invest in yourself. If you have a business plan, want to become a successful entrepreneur one day, or maybe you want to invest in shares on the stock market or whatever, this goes towards that plan.

This money will set you on a path of financial freedom to absolute abundance. This will allow you to not live the same life every single day for the rest of your life. This is what draws the line. For me personally, it was the best decision I ever made. It allowed me to invest in myself and realize what my true potential was. I am now better for it.

## 4.     Education

Absolutely, this is extremely important, If not the most important of them all. This 10% will potentially pay for a university degree or for your driving lessons and your test, depending on what your plan is. Perhaps, you aspire to become the manager at your workplace. This money in the future will pay for your certificates and licenses to allow you to move the rungs of leadership ladder. Knowledge is power and that is most definitely true. I hold that as humans, we have the potentials to develop and learn so much that we, as a race haven't even explored the surface of what is possible. So why would we just stop?

Nothing on this earth is ever constant or the same forever- is either growing or it is dying. If you are not growing, then you are inevitably dying and that is a thought nobody likes to sincerely consider.

Whatever your dream is, whatever your vision for the future could be, the knowledge and education you get will take you there.

5.      Fun

What is life without fun? You should take time out to enjoy yourself once in a while. Work is a routine which easily becomes monotonous if we don't spice it up with fun here and there- spend time chilling out, go to the cinema, buy that pair of trainers that you want and so on. It is however imperative to always remember that all that falls within the 10 percent. You must never exceed this. This is the point you learn self-restraint first hand. I really failed in this aspect and it ruined me. I became somewhat obsessed with online shopping; every payday, I would spend half my wages on ridiculous items just to give myself instant gratification. What completely eluded me was that I was wasting what could have been my future investments.

That was a hard lesson for me and if it is only one lesson you would pick from this e-book, let it be this. You must not overspend on yourself all in one go- It is irresponsible. It is ruinous!

6.      Gifts

I don't go out and pretend it is Christmas every month. You know why? It is because it really is not! Gifts include the money you spend on other people- your boyfriend, girlfriend, best friend, relatives- and even charity that you give the needy. Admittedly, you will receive if you give, we must however not forget that restraining ourselves not to put our eggs in one basket by actively saving for the future opens doors to new, potentially life-changing opportunities- it sets in motion chains of change. You cannot be living every day the same way; we would wallow in poverty.

People who get rich quick hoard their money and become ridiculously selfish and materialistic. Yet, they don't realize that by not sharing just that small percentage of their money, they are closing themselves off from the world and the people that care about them.

This is a system that you must get used to before you leave the comfort of your parent's house. It is a lot harder to start this after you have taken up responsibilities and are already paying for expenses. This will enable you make impact and live a happy, fulfilling life after you leave home.

Live through this lifestyle and allow it to become second nature. Buying piggy banks to save your money monthly could be an option. Opening different savings accounts with your bank is not a bad idea either. Choose whatever works for you. It is flexible. Advances in technology have made these transactions easier. Therefore, there is no excuse whatsoever not to execute this plan.

As a personal example, I have four different bank accounts and a piggy bank in my kitchen into which my girlfriend and I deposit our holiday money. We are saving to go abroad for the first time. You should too!

Get used to whatever works for you and practice it well. You will be in the strongest position possible whenever you want to leave home. This will also show a great level of strength from you to your parents. For your information, this transition is more stressful for them than it ever will be for you.so, you have to be meticulous about the whole process.

# Step 2: Choosing Your Roommate

This is a step that you may not have considered but ultimately would be a very wise decision to start off with.

As you can see from Step 1, the cost of Living can be straining if you are moving out on your own. There are so many expenses to contend with. Depending on your monthly wage, the responsibilities could become overwhelming if not properly managed. It saves you a heavy burden if you get a reasonable and responsible roommate who can share the burdens with you.

Sharing an apartment with a friend has lots of benefits. Having a friend or partner as your roommate will significantly enable you to split your bills and leaves you more money to save for yourself and to channel towards your own personal goals.

Quoting an Article Published online by The Independent on the 8th of November 2017, "Data shows one in four people aged 20-34 still living at home, with young men considerably more likely to be doing so than young women".

Take that as you may, but to me, this shows that currently, it is becoming more and more difficult for millennials to leave Home and make a success of it.

Majority of young people who leave home find themselves back, living with their parents within 3 months according to the UK Census figures. I left home on my own and, in all honesty, if it wasn't for the support I got from my parents financially, I too would have been back in with my parents in that time-frame.

My advice to you therefore is that, unless you have at least £1,000 left after basic deductions (spent on necessities) have been made, then it is in your best interest to consider finding a roommate to share you're the burden of bills with.

Your roommate should be somebody that you can trust, somebody who is like-minded when it comes to finances, and somebody that has ideally been in working continuously for at least 3 months prior to making the Decision.

This may sound tedious, but it is extremely important to critically consider and use as basis for any partnerships you wish to make in this regard. And that is if you really want to make things work for yourself. I am certain however certain that the last thing you will want to deal with is somebody who blasts all their wages in the first week and then leaves you to pay their half of the rent or mortgage.

If you are in a relationship and are considering moving out with a lover, it is important to note that this process is rough, full of ups and downs. Unless both of you are capable of working together as two halves of the same whole, you should alternatively consider moving out with a friend first. You can then have your partner visit you every weekend. This way you will be able to manage your finances and savings but still be able to commit to each other and everyone will be happy. Later when you have consistently saved and now have the financial clout, you can move on to a new home you're your lover while your partner gets another roommate. Alternatively, your roommate could find someone else to move out with while your partner comes in to stay with you.

A huge part of living independently is being able to juggle situations like these and make wise decisions. The reality is, as soon as you leave your parents, life confronts you with serious situations which to solve, you must be brave. These decisions, which you must tackle head-on, would surely affect your life, both short-term and in the long run.

It is important to state that you need to include your roommate in each decision that you want to make to your home. This is key to avoiding conflict. It induces the spirit of shared responsibility and cohesion. It enables you work efficiently as a team and achieve the essence of having a roommate in the first place- ease.

## 1.    Never Be the Sole Account Holder

Remember, having your name on any account makes it your legal responsibility. You don't want to be stuck with any debts if someone leaves without paying their share. Your Internet supplier does not care that the person you moved out with has broken up with you and moved halfway across the country to join a marching band.

My advice on the subject is to split the accounts.

If you pay for Gas, have your roommate pay for Electricity. If you pay for the television license, have your roommate pay for the Water Bill. This way things are shared but still legally accounted for, but remember, you must have both names on the accounts for all bills. If you pay Council-

Tax and only tell them one person lives in the house, they can take you to court for fraud because a lot of the time, companies offer discounts for single people living on their own. Where I live, I have a 10% discount on my Council-Tax. But if I moved my girlfriend in with me, I would have to notify the council. If not, they will sue me from the day she moved in.

This takes me to the Plus-One Rule; prior to moving out, set boundaries with your roommate:

• **How long can a partner stay over before they must start contributing to the bills?**

This is important because it could potentially result in you taking the slack for two people only paying 50% of the bills. That is certainly not a situation you will want to find yourself in. Therefore, after you have found your roommate, establish a list of boundaries such as the one explained above. You might even go as far as printing your own document with your signatures for the record.

If you are both going to do this, it must be fair or it will result in a fall-out that can ruin your friendship or relationship. And remember, your relationship with the people closest to you is far more valuable than any house or apartment or any form of material possessions because the memories endure forever.

## 2.    Always Have A Back-up Plan

Change is the only constant thing in this world. You may hate to consider this, but it is the reality. It is highly possible. Moving out with a friend or partner is always fun but know that the relationship could get sour. And if you do not want to be stuck with someone you resent so much, ask yourself these questions:

• If this person walks away and leaves me to pick up their side of the agreement, what would I do?

• If I lose my job, how will I pay my half of the bills?

• What if I get evicted, where will I go?

# Step 3: Finding Your First home

Once you have your budget you can start to look for your first home.

Register with the local Estate Agents online to get email notifications. This will enable you act quickly when something comes through that catches your eye.

**Research the Location**

Once you have an area in mind, do your research, online and in person. You should visit the area at different times of the day and at different times of the week to get a feel for what living in this area might be like. You might want to go the extra mile and try speaking with the neighbors. There is nothing worse than moving into your house and then quickly finding out you are living next door to a party house.

I am now in my second house after my contract ended in my first, and both times I have been lucky with my neighbors. I knew the area well. I moved not far from my parents' house and therefore knew who lived in both houses. For me, it worked to my advantage and it has made all the difference.

I wake up for work at 05:30 every morning and there have been times when neighbors down the street have kept me awake until early hours partying. If that was next door to me, I would have gone crazy!

Remember to ask yourself these questions whilst you are on the hunt.

1.      How easily can I get to work from here?

2.      How close are the local shops, and what time do they close?

3.      Are there any schools nearby that might cause traffic issues?

If you are renting your first home, then remember who the boss is!

It is always worth keeping in mind that by renting an apartment, you are paying to live in somebody else's house. This gives you your freedom, but it also carries a lot of restrictions. So, make sure you always read carefully through the Tenancy Agreement before signing. You never know what hidden restrictions you may be appending your signature to. For me, I always wanted a dog because I'm a huge dog lover and in my first house I wasn't allowed to keep pets of any shape or size. That was partly why I left the house to where I am allowed a dog. I rescued an amazing yellow Labrador who is my best friend and has seen me through all of my troubles.

Tenancy Agreements generally consist of a big list of 'What not to do's.

- Don't decorate

- Don't make much noise

- Don't alter anything

- Don't make a mess

- Don't remove anything

Generally, the property needs to be left in the exact same condition that it was met.

That takes me swiftly onto what is known by landlords as a Bond.

A Bond is a security deposit paid at the start of the tenancy.

The Bond is paid back to the tenant when they vacate the property, being that the rent has been paid in full and that there are no damages done. Any additional costs the landlord incurs due to your actions will be taken out of the Bond and you may be left with no Bond at all.

This was the case in my first house because I decided to wallpaper one wall and left it that way. They kept my entire £500 Bond to rectify it.

Therefore, be vigilant when signing your contract. Know the dos and don'ts.

Additionally, some Landlords will ask for a second Bond to be paid if you wish to keep a pet in the house, for instance. This is however at the discretion of the Landlord and is not a mandatory option.

If you do wish to have a pet when you move into your home, then notify the landlord when you first make contact. Sometimes if you are lucky, they might not even want an additional bond.

In Chapter 5, I will delve into finances and include costs of Bonds and Mortgages.

Without further ado, let's move on!

When you are on your property hunt, be sure to view a good number of properties. It is always easy to fall in love with the very first house or apartment you walk into and picture the empty carcass full of your own furniture.

However, prior to your viewing, they have been dressed to impress. The agent has run around with air freshener and gone on a cleaning frenzy, getting that house as spotless as possible. It is also a bad idea to ask the agents about the area because they just researched and would definitely provide you with positive answers. It is a job you will have to embark on yourself. You can just go out once in a while and observe what the area looks like at different times of the day and different periods of the year. Ask around. You don't want to depend on the information provided by someone whose job is to sell you something.

This is where you reel it in and be firm with the agent. Their job relies on you saying yes. So, they will be pulling every card out on you, always put them on hold and leave with a subtle "Thank you, I'll be in touch".

Go Home and create a list of potential properties that you have viewed and decide on the most suitable for you. At this point, you have viewed as many as possible and broadened your horizons enough to be able to see the bigger picture.

Start narrowing down to your final one. You should know what you like in an apartment and what you can't compromise. You should know your taste of and preferences. All of these are what you will consider before you choose where to go. And if you are 100% sure that this is going to be the home inside which to live the next chapter of your life, then it is time to give the agent the call.

The agent will invite you to meet either in their office or at the house.

And they will have a wad of paperwork for you to sign. And at this point, you have to be very careful.

This will include a full inventory checklist of the condition of every item inside the property from Carpets to Door handles and a photo to go with them.

This serves as proof lest you damage anything and, of course, they need to take you to court for not paying for the damages.

If you are buying your house, this process will be followed with the homeowner and it consists primarily of an exchange of deeds all done through a solicitor.

Then comes the Tenancy Agreement, which you need to read carefully. Take all the time that you need. I'm sure you don't need me to tell you to read before you sign!

And this will be where you will pay your first month's rent and your initial Bond Security Deposit (I will cover these in Chapter 5).

There will be an exchange of signatures and you will be handed your keys. And if you are on Meters for your Gas and Electricity, you will be given your card and key for those as well with all the details of the energy suppliers.

A brief handshake and voila you now have the very first home of your own!

Now let's get you moved in!

# Step 4: Moving Into Your New Home

After you have finally got your first apartment, the very first call for you to make is to an internet provider because they are going to take a couple of weeks establishing a connection with your home. I wager you don't want to live in a house without internet connection. That will be a cave!

1.      **Connect your Internet:** As you already know that in 2018, not many things are kept offline anymore. Almost everything you do is tracked through emails, and online data.

And of course, how can anyone live without Netflix?!

You may decide to have a contract phone with unlimited data, but my advice would be to go with an internet provider on unlimited broadband through your house because it is just so much more convenient, especially when friends come visiting.

This will also set you up with a landline number and enables you get voicemails whilst you are at work.

Living in a house without internet can be very frustrating and inconvenient. So, save yourself the hassles and book early.

**2.     Connect your Energy:** When you move to a new house, you need to disconnect the energy from the previous tenants' name and reconnect it in your own name. The process is very simple; you just call your energy provider, give them your address, the date that you are planning to move, and contact numbers. They will ask if you want your bills to be online or through the post.

My advice would be to set everything up as a direct debit through your bank so that it comes out as close to your payday as possible.

It is important that you do this just before you move so that the previous tenants won't be charged for your energy and vice versa.

**3.     Update friends and family with your new contact information**

Although it is important to change your address with the relevant businesses such as your bank and your employer, you should not forget to update your friends and relatives. Send a text and let people know your new address so that the important people in your life can get in touch with you when you start living at your new home. This will also show they are important in your life. The sense of mental closeness binds you together. With this, you will have advisers with quality experience on the journey you just started. You will have shoulders to lean on in times of need. Building this relationship and ensuring its continuity is key.

## 4.      Change your Address

It's best to do this as soon as you move in so that you don't have to rely on your parents forwarding all your mails to you.

Notify businesses and government bodies individually and promptly to make sure your mail is forwarded to the right address.

**Don't forget to:**

- Contact your car insurance provider

- Update your electoral roll details

- Let your bank know you've moved

## 5.      Additional utilities

If you want to watch a television in the UK, you must by law have a television license to allow you watch BBC on the television. So basically, if you plan on having a television you by law must have the corresponding license. This is a basic need that cannot be ignored. You don't want to be in the dark as regards what is happening in your country or environment and you don't want to miss all the real-time fun. As of now in 2018, a license costs £150 for the full year. This can however be broken down into monthly payments.

To find this, search in your web browser, www.tvlicencing.co.uk/Buy/TVLicence

## 6.    Have the new house professionally cleaned

Most properties will be given a professional clean before you viewed the house in the first place, but this means the house could have been empty for an extended period- meaning it will need another cleaning before you move in.

You can hire professionals or if you like, DIY (Do It Yourself). But while the house is empty is your best chance at getting every nook cleaned out and spotless. It makes you start on a healthy note. Health is wealth, they say. By cleaning it, you are sure there are no contractible infections or diseases around there.

## 7.      Have spare keys cut

Do this as soon as you are handed the keys to your new house.

Moving days are stressful and busy so it's very easy for keys to get lost or locked inside the house especially before you have established a key routine at your new house.

Have a new key cut for each member of the household and then a set cut for family members and a set for a trusted neighbor in case you lose your keys while out.

## 8.      Move-in Day

This is the most satisfying part of the whole process. This is what we all have been waiting for. To build the dream cave, our bachelors pad, whatever it is, it is a truly great feeling. It is a day with so much excitement and dread. You are excited you will soon be an independent adult with his own full privacy. You also dread the unknown.

You are in your apartment and now you realize that you have no furniture.

Not to worry, parents are a great source of unwanted bedsheets, cutleries and other utensils. In fact, you will fill your kitchen cupboards with pots and pans before the day is through.

Go on eBay or Facebook and find second-hand furniture; all you need to start with is a bed, a wardrobe, a sofa and a television. Everything else will likely be donated to you through friends and family. It is one of the many benefits of having a strong bond with them.

I've been living on my own for 5 years now and I still have people who give me furniture from time to time.

If you are a forward thinker (unlike me at that time), then you would have saved enough money to buy furniture and other necessities while you're still living with your parents.

Remember you will need a washing machine and an oven as well. These are worth buying before you leave home.

To move in, find a van. You can hire a man-with-a-van online. Alternatively, if you have a friend or relative with a big car with enough space and is really patient, you can do it that way as well. The beauty of leaving your parents' house is being able to fit all your life belongings in the boot of a large car.

This is a good time to have a proper clean out to get rid of any unwanted clothing. The books and other belongings you have been thinking of how to dispose could be done away with now because you will want to start on a clean slate.

## 9.    Pack a 'First Night' Bag

This will be your first night sleeping in your new home and it is really a wonderful experience. The 'big' move will have you all excited. The whole experience of living in your new home is great but look around and you will discover there is still something missing. There is no food! Preparing for your new apartment has to be as meticulous as possible that it should include how and what you will do on the first night. Being this thorough will make the transition smooth and seem effortless.

So, be sure to pack up a bag full of food for one night. Also remember to keep a change of clothes, basic toiletries, toilet paper, towels, bed sheets and any other essentials. For me, a loaf of bread, a kettle and a toaster were all the essentials I needed.

It makes such a big difference on your first night when you want to brush your teeth before bed and don't have to spend half an hour rummaging through boxes trying to find some toothpaste.

# Step 5: Finances

"Should I rent, or should I buy?" is a question you have most likely been thinking a lot about. Buying a house or a flat is one of the biggest financial decisions that you'll make. Therefore, it is important to get it right. Many people do not critically assess their worth and needs well before taking these decisions. There is no one-size-fits-all approach to this. You don't because your friend just bought a house and you also just got some money, then buying a house is the next thing. It is not a decision you jump on a bandwagon for. 'To buy or to rent' is a decision that has to be thought through before you take. If this is done wrongly, it will be regretted for life.

**Mortgage vs. Rent**

It's important to weigh up the pros and cons of buying a house as it's a huge decision that will affect you for a very long time. You have to consider your own realities and needs, not what others around you are doing or saying. It is strictly a personal decision.

Benefits of owning:

- Once you have paid off your mortgage the home will be yours and you won't have to worry about paying for somewhere to live.

- If your home increases in value, you can use the equity (its market value) to help buy a bigger home.

- You don't have to ask permission from a Landlord.

- A lot of the time, it is cheaper monthly than renting.

Potential downsides of owning:

- It's a big commitment. You need to be sure you will have sustainable income for the rest of your life.

- When interest rates rise, your monthly payments will too. It's important to be prepared for a rise.

- It can be a struggle to sell your home. You're not guaranteed a quick and easy sale.

- You need to be sure you can afford maintenance costs such as a broken boiler or burst pipes.

- If you are living with somebody and break up, deciding what to do with the property can be complicated and costly.

**Can you afford to buy?**

The first step towards buying your own home is working out your income to know whether you can afford it. You have to be as realistic as possible. You don't buy an apartment and run into debts afterwards. That doesn't make sense. Work out your finances, deduct the price of the house and see what you have left. It is a conscious decision.

If you buy a home, you'll have to pay for:

- Deposit (10% of the house price)

- Survey cost

- Stamp duty

- Removal costs

- Legal fees

- Your monthly bills

Government helps to buy

If you are on a low income or only have a small savings deposit, there are housing schemes through the government that will help you get home ownership.

This can include a 50% contribution towards your deposit or being more lenient with credit checks. You should research the ones you consider appropriate and whose payment plan is sustainable.

Let's switch to renting. Follow me, please!

**Benefits of Renting:**

• Renting allows you to move as many times as needed before settling down.

• As a tenant, the landlord is the one that will pay for property taxes, maintenance and repairs.

• You can establish a good credit history by renting a property.

• No mortgage payments to worry about.

• Opportunity to invest the money that you would have to use as a down payment for a house.

**Potential Downsides of Renting:**

•       Trouble with children, source of noise and damage from the standpoint of many landlords, giving a landlord a good reason to evict you if you make the slightest problem.

•       Inability to make changes in decoration or other aspects of the house without the landlord's permission.

•       The possibility of having to move on after a contract comes to an end.

Without any inkling of doubt, buying a house gives you the advantage of owning the most valuable asset that you would ever buy in life. But a property doesn't come on its own. It brings mortgages, taxes and more.

Renting a home, on the other hand, often saves people from the hassles. Although the drawback is not owning the house you live in.

**Savings**

As I mentioned in Step 1, Savings is at the heart of the whole process.

The bottom line is that any solid financial plan rests on a foundation of liquid assets, such as cash and money in your bank account.

Your bank account may house your everyday expenses but there are good reasons to have extra money in other savings accounts as I explained earlier.

As promised, here is my personal system of saving that has worked pretty well for me;

1.    On payday, I immediately remove 20% of my wage and transfer it into my secondary bank account- my initial 'long-term savings' account.

2.    I then halve the transferred money and send one half into my third bank account- my 'Emergency savings' account.

I am always left with 80% of my salary after these first deductions. I use this to procure my necessities and to pay my bills. I also do my food shopping with this money. The remainder is always kept in my bank account to roll over into next month. Any expenses such as going on a date night or buying a new pair of trainers and so on are taken care of from this remainder. A habit I have developed over time and which I believe is worth emulating is tracking and writing down how much gets spent and on what, allowing myself only 10% and another 10% to be spent on 'Gifts' such as going out on date night my beautiful girlfriend.

I also have a very basic spreadsheet printed out and hung up in my kitchen. I register on it every day what I have spent and on what. Being in debt made this imperative for me. I had no choice. I needed to be conscious of my spending. You shouldn't lead the hard way too. Plan well before leaving. I would suggest proper monitoring so that you don't go outside of the 10% spending margins on yourself, on others and in savings accounts. Planning for rainy days is saves you from unexpected predicaments. It provides cushion effects when you get hit with an unexpected bill. And believe me, you need to ensure that you have enough money put aside to cover it.

As I mentioned, I have a sealed piggy bank in my kitchen which my girlfriend and I put our spare change into. This is very good practice and something I do recommend. We are going on our first holiday next year and this piggy bank will not be opened until the week prior to our departure and by then I should have had two piggy banks full of change we could spend on while in Spain.

I believe for us to be able to grow, we first need to be able to love and enjoy ourselves. It is really healthy and refreshing to be able to treat yourself occasionally or else, you going to work just becomes monotonous and repetitive. And when it gets to that, life becomes drab.

Allow yourself 10% of your monthly wage and treat yourself with it. This is an amount of money that you can spend without being affected negatively in any way. So, treat yourself to a Starbucks or whatever your heart desires. Just don't be irresponsible.

Remember the 10% gift allowance? Spend it judiciously. Taking a loved one out for date night once a month (this is also treating yourself), for instance, also falls into this category. So, reap the benefits of your labour and get that supersized steak!

Managing finances is not a rigid process. It is definitely flexible. You will learn your own way of managing your finances while living on your own. These are just guidelines to give you an idea of what it looks like and put you through the process. It has worked successfully for me and for a few other people that I have shared it with. I advise you give it a try and if it is not entirely what you need, you can adjust till you get the perfect match that works best for you. It is now certain that it is a template you can bank on your way to financial freedom.

# What they don't teach in school

In this part, having got this far, I think it's time for me to unwind a little and expound a little on some important things you, most likely, have no idea about. These are the things they don't teach in schools. You learn them from experience.

For me, living on my own is a journey full of new insights and realities. You learn on it every day. Till today, I still call my mother to ask her questions like, "How do I cook a lasagna?" or "What temperature do I wash whites on?" It is definitely a continuous project.

Here are a few of the things I have learnt over the past few years. I believe they will come handy on your journey

1.      Don't close the door unless your keys are in your hand. This way you know you have them every time you leave.

2.      Keep a fire extinguisher around and learn how to use it lest there are emergencies.

3.      Put an automatic sensor bell on the front door. If you're expecting a friend over, it's a good indication that they have invited themselves in while you're upstairs. It is really important.

4.      Always keep a drawer full of medicine and a well-kept first aid kit just in case of medical exigencies.

5.      Always keep a torch to hand. If you live somewhere where power-cuts are frequent, this will be a big help when stuck in the dark.

6.      Always keep fly-killer spray in the cupboard. The day you realize what happens when you leave a window open with the light on will be an eye opener, to say the least. This will come useful a great deal.

7.      Invest in a toolkit. Just a small one with the basics will do (hammer, pliers, screwdrivers, tape measure, and allen keys). It will always come in handy. Always.

8.      Try and keep friendly with your neighbors. If like me, you have thin walls, it's important to keep the noise down on both sides. One of my neighbors understands this and the other one neighbor is quickly learning this, to say the least. It takes time and patience to communicate these preferences.

9.	Always keep the doors and windows locked. My friends are always moaning at me for locking the door every time I go through it. It is a habit I've formed an, who knows, it could have saved me from being robbed! I guess I'll never know. It is just a precautionary measure that costs you nothing. It is better safe than sorry, they say.

10.	If you have a home security system, use it. You just never know. It might come handy when you never expect.

11.	If like me, you are not the most enthusiastic cleaner, invite your friends around for a chat and a games night. It will motivate you to get the place cleaned up! Working together as a group makes the work easier and merrier!

12.	Keep your parents in the loop. They will be very worried about you, and for the first few weeks they'll probably be at your new home more than you are. It is the care and concern they have for you that makes them want to see you always. It is a strong bond they have built over the years. But once that phase passes, always keep them updated. Nobody will ever support you more than them.

13.    And most importantly, enjoy your space! After all, you are paying for the luxury. Your apartment shouldn't be a prison where you have limited freedom. Explore and make the most of it. It should bring you tranquility and, at the same time, fun.

# Good luck!

This guide is a critical analysis of the first-hand experience I had while I began my independent life journey. I wrote it to offer most strategic pieces of advice I wish I had access to while I was to set on the path. It is definitely a useful and dependable book that will help millennials transit to an independent life. It will also give the parents joy to see their children go through the transition process smoothly.

To me, you, the reader, are my younger self.

Thank you for taking the time to read through it. I heartily appreciate. And I hope it helped you as much as it has helped me just writing it! Reflections on how I started and the challenges I faced together with how I conquered them in itself are really fulfilling.

Remember, most importantly, do not overspend on unnecessary items. And always keep your parents up to date with whatever you are doing. This is the 50-million-dollar advice. Grab it now!

My name is Patrick Evans and this is my **'No-Nonsense: A Millennials Guide on How to Leave Your Parents House'**

Made in the USA
San Bernardino, CA
20 December 2018